W9-BRW-508

THE BANTAM LIBRARY
of Culinary Arts™

SPICES
roots & fruits

JILL NORMAN

BANTAM BOOKS

TORONTO · NEW YORK · LONDON · SYDNEY · AUCKLAND

SPICES: ROOTS & FRUITS

A BANTAM BOOK/PUBLISHED BY ARRANGEMENT WITH
DORLING KINDERSLEY LIMITED

PRINTING HISTORY
DORLING KINDERSLEY EDITION
PUBLISHED IN GREAT BRITAIN IN 1989

BANTAM EDITION/MAY 1989

EDITOR GWEN EDMONDS
DESIGNER JOANNA MARTIN
PHOTOGRAPHER DAVE KING

ART DIRECTOR STUART JACKMAN

ALL RIGHTS RESERVED
COPYRIGHT © 1989 BY JILL NORMAN.
ILLUSTRATIONS COPYRIGHT © 1989 DORLING KINDERSLEY.
NO PART OF THIS BOOK MAY BE REPRODUCED OR TRANSMITTED IN ANY FORM OR
BY ANY MEANS, ELECTRONIC, OR MECHANICAL, INCLUDING PHOTOCOPYING,
RECORDING, OR BY ANY INFORMATION STORAGE AND RETRIEVAL SYSTEM,
WITHOUT PERMISSION IN WRITING FROM THE PUBLISHER. FOR INFORMATION
ADDRESS:
DORLING KINDERSLEY LIMITED, 9 HENRIETTA STREET, LONDON WC2E 8PS.

LIBRARY OF CONGRESS CATALOGUING-IN-PRODUCTION DATA

NORMAN, JILL.
SPICES: ROOTS & FRUITS.
(THE BANTAM LIBRARY OF CULINARY ARTS).
INCLUDES INDEX.
I. SPICES. 2. COOKERY. I. TITLE. II. SERIES.
TX406.N685 1989 641.3'383 88-7725
ISBN 0-553-05379-5

BANTAM BOOKS ARE PUBLISHED BY BANTAM BOOKS, A DIVISION OF BANTAM
DOUBLEDAY DELL PUBLISHING GROUP, INC. ITS TRADEMARK, CONSISTING OF THE
WORDS "BANTAM BOOKS" AND THE PORTRAYAL OF A ROOSTER, IS REGISTERED IN
U.S. PATENT AND TRADEMARK OFFICE AND IN OTHER COUNTRIES. MARCA
REGISTRADA. BANTAM BOOKS INC., 666 FIFTH AVENUE, NEW YORK, NEW YORK
10103

PRINTED AND BOUND IN HONG KONG

0 9 8 7 6 5 4 3 2 1

C O N T E N T S

INTRODUCTION

Spice chest

*S*PICES ARE THE DRIED AROMATIC ROOTS, *barks, berries, and other fruits or seeds, usually of tropical plants. Most spices are native to the East, but allspice and chilies are native to tropical America and were brought east only after Columbus.*

Spices have always had great commercial value, and because of this their history has been complicated and often bloody. Caravan routes from the Far East to Europe go back at least 5000 years. The Egyptians used aromatics for embalming, for perfume, and to fumigate their homes. The Phoenicians traded spices for salt and tin along the Atlantic coast of Europe. The first real masters of the spice trade were the Arabs; Pliny complained that spices sold in Rome for a hundred times their original cost because of the Arab monopoly. Still, the Roman empire did much to spread their use, and after the fall of Rome the trade was severely curtailed until the Muslim empire spread through the Middle East and the Mediterranean, making trade routes safe again and establishing new markets. The Genoese and the Venetians, the main seafarers of the Mediterranean, vied for the trade into Europe, but the Venetians soon controlled the trade completely.

The new seaborne powers, Portugal and Spain, were intent on breaking the Venetian monopoly by establishing trade routes independent of the traditional landline to the Middle East. In 1498 Vasco da Gama found the sea route to India via the Cape of Good Hope, the Portuguese conquered the Spice Islands and made themselves

masters of a lucrative spice traffic. When the Dutch managed to oust
the Portuguese, Dutch overland trade routes into mainland Europe
became a match for the Venetian network. By the end of the 16th
century (the price of

Capsicums
Medical Botany 1834–6
Stephenson & Churchill

pepper having more than doubled in a few years) the British entered the fray, but their East India Company made little headway. The Dutch controlled the trade in cloves, mace, and nutmeg. The Portuguese still controlled cinnamon. Only slowly, as the Dutch strength in the Far East declined and the British empire began to grow, did the East India Company's fortunes improve. Six years before Vasco da Gama reached the Far East, Columbus made landfall in America, but he never did find the pepper he had set out in search of, although Mexico gave Europe a

number of useful additions to its diet: chilies, chocolate, the tomato,
and scores of lesser plants. The colonial powers began to introduce
spices to the newly opened western tropics: ginger to Mexico and the
West Indies, nutmeg and clove trees to Mauritius and Zanzibar. By
the end of the 18th century the new plantations were flourishing to the
point where no European country had a monopoly on anything
anymore, and prices started to fall. Today our spices come from all
parts of the tropics, and such is world demand that they usually are the
main exports of the producing countries.

ALLSPICE

Pimenta dioica is a small bushy tree of the myrtle family. Native to the West Indies, Central, and South America, it now grows in many tropical countries.

Its berries are picked green and when dried in the sun for about a week they turn a reddish brown. The English name reflects the curious taste, like a peppery compound of cloves, cinnamon, and mace. In many other languages it is still known by its original name, Jamaica pepper, and Jamaica is indeed the main producer.

Allspice is best stored whole, as it is quite easy to powder in a mortar or a pepper mill. Whole, it is one of the common pickling and marinading spices, but ground it is popular in cakes. It is a standard ingredient in many commercial sauces and ketchups.

Pimenta dioica

CLOVES

EUGENIA·CARYOPHYLLUS originated in the Moluccas, the fabled Spice Islands of Indonesia, and was the mainstay of the Portuguese and Dutch spice monopoly. It is now cultivated on the African islands, especially Zanzibar, and in the West Indies.

Clove trees are evergreens of the myrtle family. They bear fruit within ten years of planting and easily live to around 60. The pinkish buds are picked just before they open; dried in the sun for four or five days they turn a reddish brown. The central part is easy to grind to a powder. Ground cloves keep their pungent taste better than most ground spices. Cloves are an important ingredient of curry powders, garam masala, and of sweet mixtures used for cakes.

Eugenia caryophyllus

CHILIES

*C*HILIES, CAPSICUM FRUTESCENS *and C. annuum, have been cultivated in South America for at least 5000 years. The Aztecs used pickled chilies and chili powder – we owe them the name. After Columbus the fruit spread through Europe and into every part of the Spanish and Portuguese colonial empires: West Africa, India, southeast Asia, Indonesia, the Philippines. The Italians sold them to the Turks, the Turks spread them through the Balkans, and the Persians took them to northern India and Kashmir.*

Chilies added a powerful spice and a cheap vegetable to the global diet. They belong to that bountiful group of New World nightshades that includes the potato and the tomato.

They like heat, and will grow well in altitudes of 6–7000 feet (2000 m).

cherry

guajillo

bird's eye

serrano

The vast number of different chilies is due partly to stable hybrids produced by cross-pollination and partly to cultivation.

The smaller the chili and the thinner its flesh, the more elongated its shape, and the sharper the end, the hotter it will be. Color is no guide, for although green chilies are unripe and the red, yellow, or purple ones mature, this affects the flavor (which becomes stronger, as in all fruit) but not the heat.

ancho

crushed chili

cayenne

chili flakes

paprika

lombok

CHILI VARIETIES

ANCHO: triangular, 3 by 4 inches (8 by 10 cm), reddish-brown when dried; mild and rich. When green it is called poblano, looks much like a bell pepper, and is used as a vegetable, stuffed. The classic pepper of Mexico.

BELL: broad and squarish, 3–4 inches (8–10 cm), green, red, or yellow; sweet and mild. The standard "sweet pepper" of Europe, the basis of Hungarian paprika powder and Spanish pimentón.

BIRD or *BIRD'S-EYE:* the smallest of all the peppers about 1 inch (2.5 cm) long, thin, pointed – and very hot.

CAYENNE: very narrow, up to 3 inches (7–8 cm) long, curved, pointed, bright red; hot. Usually found dried, or ground as the hot cayenne pepper of commerce. Grown extensively.

CHERRY: round, ½–1 inch (1–3 cm) in diameter, yellow or red; often hot when small, milder when larger. Usually sold pickled.

HABANERO: shaped like a small lantern, usually light green and fiercely hot. Scotch Bonnet in the West Indies.

HONKA: 2 inches (5 cm) long, dark or orange red; quite hot. A Japanese variety similar to cayenne. Lombok is its Malaysian and Indonesian variety.

cayenne

JALAPEÑO: 1 inch (2.5 cm) wide, and short, up to 3 inches (7–8 cm), dark green, round-tipped; hot. When dried and smoked it is called by its old Aztec name chipotle, often sold canned, and used as a fragrant but not particularly hot flavoring for soups and stews. Grown and used in South and Central America.

MULATO: 3 inches (8 cm) wide, 5–6 inches (12–15 cm) in length, brownish red to black when dried, wrinkled; pungent but not hot. Mexican.

tabasco

PASILLA: 1 inch (2.5 cm) wide, 6–7 inches (15–18 cm) long, dark, red, hot, and of rich flavor. Mexican.

SERRANO: narrow and short, up to 2 inches (5 cm), pointed, deep green when fresh, orange-red when dried; hot.

TABASCO: thin and short, 1–1½ inches (2–4 cm), pointed, bright red; very hot. Basis of tabasco sauce. Cultivated around the Gulf of Mexico.

TOGARASHI: small red peppers from Japan, very hot; sold fresh and whole, dried and flaked, or ground – the latter called ichimi.

habanero

poblano

serrano

jalapeño

11

GINGER & GALANGAL

ZINGIBER OFFICINALE has been cultivated in tropical Asia for over three thousand years and was one of the first spices to reach Europe, where it was popular during the Middle Ages. The Spaniards established its culture in the West Indies early in the 16th century and these days it grows almost anywhere in the tropics.

A perennial herbaceous plant no more than 3 feet (1 meter) high, propagated by division. The creeping rhizomes, irregular in shape, provide the spice. Fresh ginger is harvested at any time from a month after planting. Hawaii and Fiji are the great exporters of fresh ginger. The preserved ginger of Chinese origin is made by boiling very young shoots with sugar. Mature rhizomes are dried, either with the skin on and therefore rather dark, or peeled and bleached, after scalding. Dried ginger, more pungent than fresh, is used powdered or simply bruised. Most of it comes from India and Jamaica, but China seems set to over-take both. Ginger is warming, with a distinct "bite," but not "hot." Fresh ginger can be sliced and preserved in dry sherry.

Zingiber officinale

Powdered ginger

Beni-shōga

Dried ginger

Ginger breads and biscuits, beers and cordials are known the world over. Ginger is also essential in curry mixes and in China and Japan in fish dishes.

Beni-shōga, Japanese red pickled ginger, is popular with sushi.

Galangal (*Alpinia galanga*), known as laos in Indonesia and Malaysia and as khaa in Thailand, is ginger's close relative, similar in appearance and properties, if not quite as pungent, and with a slight hint of sourness which makes it less attractive for use in sweet dishes. In many parts of southeast Asia it is preferred to ginger. It was popular in Europe during the Middle Ages, but, unlike ginger, it did not retain its popularity in the West.

Galangal is still difficult to buy fresh. Dried galangal can be bought whole or powdered. The powder is used in curries and finds sporadic employ in the Middle East and North Africa. In Thailand the flowers are eaten fried, as we do zucchini flowers.

Alpinia galanga

JUNIPER

JUNIPERUS COMMUNIS *grows wild all over the northern hemisphere, in Asia, Europe, and America, and particularly in wild or mountainous regions up to considerable altitudes.*

It is a bushy evergreen of the cypress family, usually not more than 4–6 feet (120–180 cm) high. The female plant bears berries that take two years to ripen into the blue-to-purple fruit we use as a spice. Picking them is hazardous because the spiky leaves, green with a white stripe, are exceedingly sharp. Juniper varies depending on location and climate: the farther south, the taller the plant, and the stronger the bittersweet aroma of the fruit. It will grow readily in most gardens. Juniper is well known as the flavoring for many gins and cordials, and as a marinading and curing spice. The berries are usually just crushed, but may be chopped finer for use in pâté mixes and the like.

Their flavor blends well with that of the more pungent herbs, garlic, and wine or brandy as used with game and pork.

Juniperus communis

14

NUTMEG &
MACE

YRISTICA FRAGRANS is a native of the Moluccas and the Philippines. It was known in Europe in the Middle Ages but only became popular after the Portuguese developed the Spice Islands trade. In the eighteenth century it was introduced to other parts of the tropics, notably the West Indies.

Kernel

Ground nutmeg

"Nutmegs cause a sweet breath, and mend those that stink, if they be much chewed and holden in the mouth," (John Gerard's Herball. 1597).

The whole fruit

The nutmeg tree is a large tropical evergreen. The fruit looks like a yellow peach until it dries and splits open, revealing a kernel, the nutmeg, surrounded by a scarlet aril, the mace.
Nutmeg goes well with spinach and in cheese dishes. It is an essential flavoring of Middle Eastern food.
In large quantities it is toxic and has long been used as a soporific in night-time drinks.
Mace has a more genteel flavor, perfect for soups and sweet dishes. Both are better stored whole, and ground only when required.

Mace

PEPPER

*P*IPER NIGRUM *is a tropical family of perennial climbers which originated in Malabar, on the east coast of India. Their product had reached Europe overland by Greek and Roman times. Vine peppers now grow in any climate warm and wet enough. They are still the main spice of the Spice Islands, but they are equally at home in Sri Lanka, Brazil, and Madagascar.*

Piper nigrum yields not only the black pepper its name suggests, but also the green and the white. For black pepper, the berries, which are on long hanging spikes, are picked mature but still green and dried in the sun. For white, they are picked when ripe (and a light red) and their skins removed before also being dried.

Piper nigrum (vine peppers)

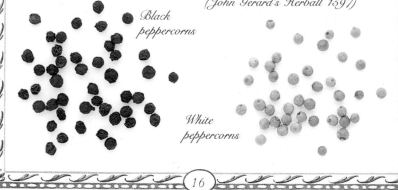

"They heate and comfort the brain,"
(John Gerard's Herball 1597)

Black peppercorns

White peppercorns

Green pepper, a very profitable addition to the range, is available in two forms: fresh berries conserved in a mild pickle, or dehydrated. The dehydrated berries can be reconstituted by steeping in water. Occasionally one finds pink pepper-corns, which are ripe berries treated in the same two ways.

Obviously, pepper is best bought whole, and ground only as and when required. For cooking, a peppermill stocked with a mixture of black and white corns is very useful.

Black and white pepper both have a very pungent, biting taste – black a little coarser but also milder, white preferred for such dishes as might look odd with dark specks.

Fresh green pepper has a very similar taste but is less hot.

There has been a curious change in the use of the two "pepper" families. Originally, the *piper* variety provided the bite in the curry mixes of India, but since the introduction of the *capsicums* from America these have taken over.

Green peppercorns

Piper longum

Cubeba officinalis

Piper longum from India is long pepper once much liked in Europe but now used only in the Far East. Cubebs are the berries of *Cubeba officinalis*, a native of Java. They have a pungent, spicy flavor rather more bitter than that of the peppers.

SAFFRON

*C*ROCUS SATIVUS *originated in Asia Minor: the Assyrians and Phoenicians used it, so did the Greeks. The Arabs had brought it to Spain by the 10th century, and it reached Britain in the 14th. For 400 years Essex was an important producer of the spice, around Saffron Walden. Today Spain is the main producer.*

The saffron crocus will grow in almost any well-drained soil, but needs sun. As soon as the lilac-colored flowers open, in autumn, the styles are picked and dried – a labor-intensive process since it takes well over a hundred thousand flowers to produce 1 lb (450 g) of saffron.

Good saffron is a reddish orange, it swells on contact with warm water and the yellow color seeps out readily. Saffron is essential to many fish dishes (bouillabaisse, zarzuela, and shellfish paella), to some risottos, and to a variety of fine breads and candies. A very small quantity will, where possible by way of an infusion, spread both the color and the pungent bitterish aroma a long way.

Crocus sativus

TURMERIC

Curcuma longa is native to southeast Asia, but it grows in most of the tropics. It made its way through India (which is now the main producer) and Arabia into Europe, and from there to America: the United States has become the largest importer.

Turmeric is a perennial plant closely related to ginger, but with large lilylike leaves. It is grown from pieces of rhizome, and it is the rhizomes that make the spice: they are boiled, then dried in the sun for about two weeks,

Curcuma longa

and finally cleaned and polished. Turmeric is usually sold ground; it retains its coloring potential indefinitely, but the same cannot be said for its characteristic rather earthy aroma.

Its earliest use may well have been as a cheap yellow dye in dry climates (to be effective elsewhere it would need a chemical fixing agent). Even in food it is often used more for its color than for its taste, for instance in mustards and commercial sauces. In curry powders both elements combine.

STAR ANISE

Illicium verum is a native of southern China and southeast Asia which has never really spread anywhere else. It seems to have been brought west by the English in the late 16th century.

It is the fruit of a small evergreen tree of the magnolia family which is picked before it is ripe, and dried. Its shape is that of a very irregular eight-pointed star. The flavor is more of licorice than of anise and has a distinct and pungent hint of sweetness. It is a standard ingredient of five-spice powder, one of the essential flavorings in Chinese cooking.

Star anise is often used whole, and a few carpels would suffice even in roasting a whole chicken. It is also the flavoring agent for many drinks of the pastis-anisette-anis family, especially the French ones.

Illicium verum

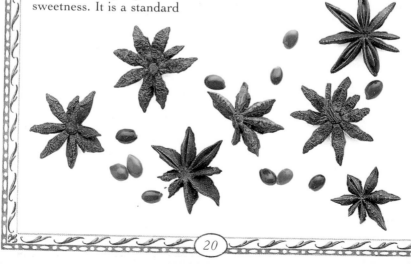

SZECHUAN PEPPER & ASAFETIDA

*X*ANTHOXYLUM PIPERITUM OR *FAGARA is known in Cantonese as* fahjiu, *"flower pepper." The berries of this small tree become highly aromatic reddish brown globes when dried. They are not "hot" but slightly numbing. They should be lightly roasted and can then be used either whole, crushed, or ground. Szechuan pepper often makes the fifth in five-spice powder (unless ginger is used instead).*

Xanthoxylum piperitum

Ferula asafoetida

Ferula asafoetida and *F. narthex* are fennels native to Iran and Afghanistan. The milky gum from the taproot of these plants dries to a pearly resin which darkens with age. Its high sulphur content makes asafetida smell foul (hence names like devil's dung), but used sparingly it gives a very aromatic flavor. Combined with garlic and onion it is the basis of much southern Indian vegetarian cooking.

SPICE BLENDS
of the western hemisphere

*B*LENDS OF SPICES *have been used as long as the spices themselves, and the great kitchens of the Middle Ages had developed several standard mixes. In England and France blends called* poudre blanche *were common; one recipe calls for 9 parts of ginger to 2 of cinnamon and 1 each of cloves and grains of paradise, mixed with 32 parts of sugar* (Le Ménagier de Paris, 1393).

Present-day blends, often available commercially in ready-mixed form, divide into ground ones generally used for baking and whole-spice mixtures used for pickling or in savory dishes from which they may be removed before eating.

MIXED SPICE or pudding spice *is an old English blend of allspice, cinnamon, cloves, mace, and nutmeg. Mincemeat* spice *is very similar but usually includes ginger, as does American* Pumpkin pie spice, *which leaves out the allspice.*

Ras el Hanout

Pickling spices are also found in traditional but varying blends. Two mixtures specified in Law's Grocer's Manual *(4th edition, 1950)* provide 14 lb each:

1½ lb mustard seed, 2½ lb black peppercorns, 1½ lb white peppercorns, 2 lb cayenne pods, 2½ lb pimento, 1½ lb good cloves, 2 lb Jamaica ginger, ½ lb small mace.

1¾ lb yellow mustard seed, 2¼ lb Indian black pepper, 1½ lb bird's-eye or Nyasa chilies, 3½ lb pimento, 1½ lb Zanzibar cloves, 2 lb Jamaica ginger, ¾ lb mace, ¾ lb coriander seeds.

QUATRE ÉPICES is the most widely used French spice mix. Its most common formula is 5 parts pepper to 2 of nutmeg and 1 each of cloves and ginger, but allspice, cinnamon and occasionally cayenne may be included. This blend is particularly good in long cooking stews, pâtés and other types of charcuterie.

HARISSA is a potent paste made of reconstituted dried cayenne peppers, pounded with salt, garlic, coriander, and herbs, then mixed with olive oil.

RAS EL HANOUT is a renowned Moroccan blend of a dozen or more spices, which never fails to intrigue foreign visitors. It usually contains cardamom, mace, galangal, long pepper, cubebs, nutmeg, allspice, cinnamon, cloves, ginger, rose buds, lavender flowers, ash berries, and Spanish fly. The mixture is stored whole, and ground as and when required. It is particularly good with game and some lamb dishes.

Recipes

*All recipes are for 4,
but some (such as cakes or tarts
and terrines) will serve more*

Harira

Harira is a thick creamy soup
eaten in Morocco to break the
daily fast of Ramadan.

6 oz/175 g chicken, chopped
1 onion, chopped
2 cloves garlic, chopped
3 tomatoes, peeled and chopped
2½ pints/1½ liters chicken stock
½ teaspoon ground cinnamon
½ teaspoon ground cumin
*½ teaspoon ground ras el hanout
(optional)*

*½ teaspoon ground ginger
salt*
4 oz/125 g cooked chick-peas
4 oz/125 g vermicelli
*a handful of chopped parsley or
coriander*
2 eggs
2 teaspoons harissa (optional)
1 lemon

Put the chicken, onion, garlic,
and tomatoes in a pan with the
stock, bring to the boil, and
remove any scum. Add the

spices and salt, cover the pan, and simmer for about an hour.

Add the chick-peas and vermicelli and cook for another 10–15 minutes, or until the pasta is cooked. Stir in the parsley or coriander.

Beat the eggs, remove the pan from the heat, and stir them into the soup. Stir in the harissa, or put some on the table. Serve at once with lemon wedges.

MOROCCAN EGG PASTRIES

These are small triangular or rolled pies made with filo pastry. Instead of the egg filling you could use the combination of canned tuna and egg that is popular in Tunisia.

1 small onion, chopped finely
2–3 tablespoons olive oil
1/4 teaspoon ground ginger
1/4 teaspoon black pepper
1/4 teaspoon ground allspice
1/4 teaspoon saffron threads, pounded
pinch cayenne
4 eggs
a bunch of parsley, chopped
salt
1 tablespoon lemon juice
8 oz/250 g filo pastry
4 oz/125 g butter, melted

Heat the olive oil and gently fry the onion and the spices in it for a few minutes. Beat the eggs, stir in the parsley and a little salt, and add them to the pan. Cook, stirring occasionally, until the eggs start to set (4–5 minutes). Add the lemon juice just at the end and take the pan from the heat. When it has cooled, chop the mixture. Cut the sheets of filo pastry into 3 strips; cover with a cloth to prevent them drying out. Take a strip of the pastry, brush it lightly with melted butter, and put a tablespoon of the filling near one end. Fold the corner over to make a triangle and continue folding triangles until the strip is used up; alternatively, make a roll, folding in the sides.

Put the pastries on a buttered oven tray and bake in a preheated oven, 160°C/325°F, for about 20 minutes.

HERB OMELETTE

Dishes like this, which resemble a substantial Spanish omelette, are called *kookoo* in Iran, and *eggah* in the Arab world. They can be served hot or cold, cut in wedges like a cake, accompanied by a bowl of thick yogurt. This version is an Iranian new year dish, its greenness symbolizing the coming spring.

1 leek
2–3 scallions
3–4 lettuce leaves
3–4 spinach leaves
2–3 small zucchini (optional)
3 tablespoons chopped parsley
3 tablespoons chopped mixed fresh herbs
3 tablespoons chopped dill
a handful of walnuts, chopped
a few threads of saffron
6 eggs
¼ teaspoon black pepper
salt
1 oz/25 g butter

Chop the vegetables finely and combine them with the herbs and the walnuts. Pound the saffron in a mortar, add 2 teaspoons of water, and blend. Beat the eggs well; add the saffron liquid, pepper, salt; then tip in the vegetable mixture. Pour the whole into a buttered ovenproof dish. Bake in a preheated oven, 180°C/350°F, for 40–60 minutes. The dish should be crisp at the bottom and have a light brown crust.

ᚴPICY FISH STEAKS

This recipe works well with good firm steaks of any fish. It's excellent with tuna, grouper, cod, and halibut.

4 fish steaks
1 ball of tamarind,[1] or juice of
1 lemon
peanut oil
2 fresh red chilies, seeded and sliced
1 large onion, chopped
2 cloves garlic, crushed
1 teaspoon ground galangal
2 tablespoons dark soy sauce
salt

If using tamarind, soak it in a few teaspoons of warm water until soft, then squeeze it until it absorbs the water. Use this, or the lemon juice, to marinate the fish for half an hour.

Dry the fish; fry it briefly on both sides in a little oil. Remove the fish, drain off the oil until there is only about a tablespoon of it left in the pan, then use this to fry the chilies, onion, garlic, and galangal. Add 4–5 tablespoons of water and the soy sauce, and a little salt if ecessary. Simmer for a minute or two. Put back the fish steaks, cover, and cook for 5–10 minutes until the fish is ready. Don't let it get too dry. Spoon the sauce over and serve hot.

1) Tamarind is a pleasantly sharp-tasting pulp extracted from the pods of a tropical tree, and is widely used in southeast Asian cooking. It is most conveniently bought in small balls coated with sugar.

ᚴTEAMED SALMON WITH GINGER AND LIME

Mix together *a tablespoon each of sesame oil, light soy sauce,* and *finely chopped fresh ginger* with *2 tablespoons of dry sherry*. Rub *4 salmon steaks or fillets* with this marinade, season them with *salt*, and leave for 30 minutes. Heat the water in the steamer, put the fish on a plate or a piece of foil, cover with foil or plastic wrap, and steam until the fish is firm to the touch — about 10–12 minutes. Serve with its juices, sprinkled with *grated lime peel, chopped chives,* and *wedges of lime*.

WEST INDIAN MARINATED SHRIMP

Marinate *1 lb/500 g large, cooked and shelled shrimp* for about an hour in *¼ pint/150 ml olive oil, 3 tablespoons of lime juice, a teaspoon of Worcestershire sauce,* and *2 teaspoons of tabasco,* with a little *salt.*

You can add *1 or 2 sliced avocados* just before serving, but you may then need to increase the amount of oil and lime juice. Serve as a first course.

CHINESE BRAISED FISH

1 gray mullet or sea bass of about
3 lb/1.5 kg, cleaned
3 slices fresh ginger
6 dried Chinese mushrooms
2 tablespoons sherry
2 tablespoons soy sauce
1 tablespoon honey
¼ teaspoon salt
2 tablespoons oil
2 star anise
½ pint/300 ml chicken stock or water
1 tablespoon cornstarch

Dry the fish thoroughly with paper towels. Make two diagonal slashes on both sides; rub with ginger. Soak the mushrooms in warm water for 30 minutes, then drain and chop them.

Mix together the sherry, soy sauce, honey, and salt in a bowl. Choose a wok, or a pan with a lid, big enough to hold the fish and heat the oil in it until very hot. Add the ginger and stir for a minute. Lower the heat, put in the fish, and fry for 2 minutes on each side. Pour off the oil, sprinkle the sherry mixture over the fish. Add the star anise, the mushrooms, and the heated stock or water.

Let the liquid come to the boil, then lower the heat, cover the pan, and braise the fish for 20 minutes. Turn once during cooking. When ready the fish should flake easily if tested with a fork near the backbone. Transfer the fish to a heated platter. Turn up the heat to reduce the sauce a little. Blend the cornstarch with a tablespoon of water and stir into the sauce until it thickens. Pour the sauce over the fish. Serve with rice.

Pork, Veal, and Ham Terrine

12 oz/375 g veal, minced
1 lb/500 g pork, minced
4 juniper berries, crushed
½ teaspoon mace or allspice
½ teaspoon thyme
1 clove garlic, crushed
salt and pepper
3 tablespoons brandy
2 eggs
pork fatback or bacon
12 oz/375 g lean cooked ham, cut in strips about ¼ in (5 mm) thick
1 bay leaf

Mix the veal and pork well with the herbs, spices and marinate in the brandy for an hour or two. Beat the eggs lightly, stir them into the mixture.

Line the sides and bottom of a terrine with fatback or bacon. Put in a third of the veal and pork mixture, then arrange half the ham strips in a layer. Repeat this with another third of the mixture and the rest of the ham. Cover with the remaining mixture, put a bayleaf in the center, and more fatback or bacon over the top. Cover the terrine tightly with foil and its lid, stand it in a pan of hot water, and cook in a preheated oven, 160°C/325°F, for 2 hours. Cool the terrine, remove the lid, and put a weight on top of the foil. Refrigerate for several hours before serving.

LAMB WITH APRICOT

*8 oz/250 g amardine or dried
apricots
a small shoulder of lamb
1/4 teaspoon ground ginger
1/2 teaspoon ground cinnamon
pinch ground cloves
freshly ground black pepper
salt*

If you can buy sheets of apricot paste called amardine from a Greek or oriental grocer, they make this dish very easy. Otherwise, soak dried apricots briefly, drain, and chop them finely.

Remove all fat from the lamb, and rub the flesh with the spices and a little salt. Spread the amardine or the chopped apricots over all sides of the lamb and wrap it well in a large piece of oiled foil. Put it on a baking tray into a preheated oven, 150°C/300°F.

Cook for at least 2½ hours; no harm will be done if you leave it longer. The meat should be sufficiently tender to fall off the bone rather than need carving. The juices in the package can be used as gravy for accompanying rice, or the chick-peas given on page 35 will go well with this dish.

LEAN SPICED MEATBALLS

*1 lb/500 g minced meat
4 teaspoons galangal
1½ teaspoons sambal (trassi,
preferably)
juice of 2 lemons
1 onion*

Put all the ingredients 2 or 3 times through a mincer. Roll into small balls. Steam for 20–30 minutes. The meat will lose all its fat in the process.

STUFFED CHICKEN IN CABBAGE PARCELS

8 chicken thighs, skinned and boned
2–3 dried mushrooms (porcini)
8 cabbage leaves
3 oz/75 g mushrooms
2 shallots
2 oz/50 g butter
8 juniper berries, crushed finely
salt and
pepper

Pour ¼ pint/150 ml boiling water over the dried mushrooms and leave them to soak for 30 minutes.
Remove the central stalk from the cabbage leaves, then blanch the leaves in boiling water for 5 minutes.
Chop the fresh mushrooms and shallots finely and sauté them briefly in half the butter. Season with salt and pepper and the crushed juniper berries. Drain the dried mushrooms, keeping the liquid, and chop them. Add to the fresh mushrooms and shallots, and use the mixture to stuff the chicken pieces. Wrap each piece in a cabbage leaf. Brush the parcels with melted butter and put them in a greased baking dish. Sprinkle over a little of the mushroom liquid, cover with foil, and bake in a preheated oven, 200°C/400°F, for 30 minutes.

LIVER WITH PAPRIKA

1 lb/500 g calf's liver
flour
1 tablespoon paprika
salt and pepper
2 oz/50 g butter
2 cloves garlic, crushed
a small glass of white wine
a handful of chopped parsley
1/4 pint/150 ml sour cream

Cut the liver into thin strips and coat them with flour seasoned with paprika, salt, and pepper. Melt the butter in a heavy pan and add the liver and garlic. Sauté for 2–3 minutes over high heat, turning the liver until it is evenly browned.

Take out the liver and keep it warm while you make the sauce. Add the wine and parsley to the pan, scrape loose any bits that are sticking and boil briefly. Reduce the heat and stir in the cream; heat through but do not boil. Put the liver into the sauce and serve.

DUCK BREASTS WITH GREEN PEPPERCORNS

4 duck breasts, boned
1 tablespoon oil
salt
6 tablespoons dry white vermouth
3 tablespoons chicken stock or water
1/4 pint/150 ml heavy cream
2 tablespoons green peppercorns
2 tablespoons sweet red pepper,
diced small

Remove the skin and the fat from the duck breasts and sauté them in the oil in a heavy frying pan for 6–7 minutes. Turn them over, sprinkle with salt, and cook for a further 4–5 minutes.

The meat should feel firm but still springy. Arrange the duck on a serving plate, cover, and keep warm.

Deglaze the frying pan with the vermouth and stock or water. Bring to the boil and reduce by half. Pour in the cream, season with salt, add the peppercorns, and simmer until the sauce is reduced by a third. Stir in the diced red pepper at the last moment, then pour the sauce around the duck breasts and serve.

CHILI BREAD

Pound *2 cloves of garlic* in a mortar; add *a handful of parsley* and *a small onion*, both finely chopped, and *a tablespoon of chili powder*; mix well. Add *2 tablespoons of olive oil* and *2 oz/50 g butter*; blend well, adding *salt* to taste.

Spread the mixture on *French bread* (halved lengthwise) and sprinkle with *Parmesan cheese*. Bake in a preheated oven until the mixture has melted into the bread and the edges are crisp – about 10 minutes.

ONION TART

Make a shortcrust pastry with *7 oz/225 g flour, 3 oz/75 g butter, a pinch of salt,* and a little *water.* Line an 8 in/20 cm tart pan with the pastry.

Slice *1 lb/500 g onions* thinly and cook them gently for 20 minutes in a mixture of *oil* and *butter*. Do not let them brown. Sprinkle over *a tablespoon of flour*, stir it in, and leave to cook for a few minutes more. Remove the pan from the heat and transfer the onions to the tart tin. Pour over *3/4 pint/450 ml crème fraîche* (or *cream* mixed with a little *lemon juice*) seasoned with *salt, pepper, and nutmeg*. Bake in a preheated oven 180°C/350°F, for about 30 minutes. Remove the tart from the tin and serve hot.

SHIITAKE MUSHROOMS WITH GARLIC, PEPPER, AND GINGER

12 oz/375 g fresh shiitake mushrooms
4 tablespoons oil
a small piece of fresh ginger, peeled and chopped finely
3 cloves garlic, crushed with a little salt
1 teaspoon Szechuan pepper, crushed
Chinese or ordinary chives, chopped

Wipe the mushrooms and cut them in pieces. Heat the oil in a frying pan or wok; add the ginger, garlic, and pepper; fry for a minute or two, then add the mushrooms and sauté for 4 or 5 minutes. Serve garnished with chives.

POTATOES WITH TURMERIC

An Indian dish that is very simple to make and can be served as part of a western meal.

1 lb/500 g potatoes
3–4 tablespoons oil
8 oz/250 g small onions
1 teaspoon turmeric
1/4 teaspoon asafetida (optional)
salt
1 green chili, chopped finely
1 tablespoon chopped coriander leaves

Boil the potatoes in their skins until cooked but firm. Let them cool, then peel and cut into cubes. Heat the oil in a frying pan, put in the whole onions and cook over low heat, shaking the pan frequently, for about 20 minutes. Turn up the heat, and add the turmeric, asafetida, and potatoes. Sprinkle with salt and fry, turning frequently, for 3–4 minutes. Add a couple of tablespoons of water, cover the pan and turn down the heat. Cook for a further 5 minutes; uncover, and scatter on the chopped chili and coriander. Turn up the heat to evaporate any remaining liquid, then serve.

SPICED CHICK-PEAS

8 oz/250 g chick-peas, soaked for several hours or overnight
1 onion, chopped
2 cloves garlic
a sprig of thyme
1 bayleaf
1 teaspoon ground allspice
salt

Put the chick-peas in a large pan together with the onion, garlic, herbs, and allspice. Cover with water, bring to the boil, then simmer until tender – which will take an hour or more, depending on the age of the peas and how long they were soaked. Add salt just for the last 5 minutes or so.

This dish can be prepared well ahead of whatever you may wish to use it with: the chick-peas keep and reheat well in their liquid. Remove the herbs, the peas can then be served with a just a little oil or butter. Spinach goes well with them.

DAL

An Indian lentil puree that goes
well with rice and other
vegetable dishes.

10 oz/300 g lentils
1/2 teaspoon turmeric
1/2 teaspoon salt
5 tablespoons oil
pinch asafetida
1/4 teaspoon cayenne
1 teaspoon cumin seeds
4–5 cloves garlic, sliced finely
2 red chilies, seeds removed, chopped
*2 tablespoons chopped coriander
leaves*

Pick over the lentils and, unless you are using the little red ones, put them to soak for an hour. Drain them. Put them in a pan with 1¾ pint/1 liter water, the turmeric, and salt. Bring to the boil, stirring occasionally, then lower the heat and simmer, partially covered, until the lentils become a puree or thick soup: this will take 20–45 minutes depending on the type of lentils, and you may need to add a little water in the process. Beat with a wooden spoon to make the puree smoother, put it in a serving dish, and keep warm.

Heat the oil in a large frying pan and add the asafetida, cayenne, cumin seeds, garlic and chilies. Fry until the garlic starts to color, then pour the whole over the lentils. Garnish with the coriander and serve.

VEGETABLES BRAISED IN SPICED YOGURT

2 potatoes
2–3 tomatoes
1 small eggplant
6 oz/175 g green beans
2 onions
6 oz/175 g peas, shelled
3 green chilies
oil
1/2 teaspoon turmeric
1 teaspoon ground coriander
1 teaspoon ground cumin
1/2 teaspoon chili powder
1/4 teaspoon ground cloves
a small piece of fresh ginger, peeled
and crushed
3 cloves garlic, crushed
1/2 pint/300 ml thick plain yogurt
salt

Cut the peeled potatoes, tomatoes, and eggplant into pieces of similar size; cut the beans in half. Slice the onions and fry them, with the whole chilies, in the oil until lightly browned. Add the spices and garlic, cook for a minute more, then put in the yogurt a little at a time. Stir until the mixture is well blended and thick. Turn the heat to very low, put in the potatoes, cover the pan, and cook until they are starting to soften. Add the other vegetables and a little water if necessary to prevent sticking. Season with salt, cover the pan again, and simmer for another 15–20 minutes, until all the vegetables are cooked.

FRIED TOASTS

"Chip *a manchet* very well, and cut it roundways into toasts; then take *cream* and *eight eggs*, season'd with *sack*, *sugar* and *nutmeg*; and let these toasts steep for about an hour; then fry them in *sweet butter*, serve them up with *plain melted butter*, or with *butter*, *sack and sugar*, as you please."

E. Smith, *The Compleat Housewife*, 1727 and many later editions. A manchet was white bread of the finest quality. For sack use sherry, and only make as much of the cream and egg mixture as you will need to cover your bread.

CURD CHEESECAKES

"Beat *half a pint of good curds* with *four eggs*, *three spoonfuls of rich cream*, *half a nutmeg* grated, and *a spoonful of ratafia, rose, or orange water*. Put to them *a quarter of a pound of sugar*, and *half a pound of currants* well washed and dried before the fire. Mix them all well together, put a good crust into your patty-pans, and bake them."

John Farley, *The London Art of Cookery*, 1783

CHRISTMAS STOLLEN

Stollen is a rich, spiced fruit bread traditionally made for Christmas in central Europe. Its shape is said to resemble a baby in swaddling clothes.

2 lb/1 kg flour
½ teaspoon salt
3 tablespoons dried yeast
½ pint/300 ml milk
5 oz/150 g sugar
10 oz/300 g butter
grated rind of 2 lemons
4 oz/125 g mixed candied peel, chopped
10 oz/300 g raisins
10 oz/300 g currants
4 oz/125 g blanched almonds, chopped
½ teaspoon ground cloves
½ teaspoon ground cinnamon
½ teaspoon ground mace
butter and confectioners' sugar

Sift the flour and salt into a large bowl. Dissolve the yeast in the tepid milk with 1 teaspoon of the sugar. While it is proving, melt the butter and leave to cool slightly.

Make a well in the center of the flour, pour in the yeast mixture, and beat well. Add the melted butter, the rest of the sugar, and the lemon rind. Knead for about 10 minutes, until the dough no longer looks moist or sticks to the hands or the sides of the bowl. Cover and leave to rise in a warm place until it has doubled in bulk – about 1½ hours – then punch back the dough and carefully knead in the peel, fruit, nuts, and spices. Cover again, leave to prove for another 1–1½ hours or until it has doubled in bulk.

Divide the dough in two equal parts, leave one covered while shaping the first. Roll dough into a flattened oval, make a dent lengthways with the rolling pin to one side of the center, fold the wider side over the dent. Put the stollen on a buttered baking sheet, cover, and leave to prove for 30 minutes. Make the second stollen the same way.

Bake in a preheated oven, 190°C/375°F, for about 45–60 minutes. Test with a skewer. Coat the warm stollen with melted butter and sprinkle thickly with confectioners' sugar. Wrapped well and stored in a dry place stollen will keep for several weeks.

INDEX

ACKNOWLEDGEMENTS

Bantam Books would like to thank the following people:

· ILLUSTRATORS ·
JANE THOMSON
SHEILAGH NOBLE

· MARBLER ·
SARAH AMATT

FALKINER FINE
PAPERS LTD

ROYAL BOTANICAL
GARDENS KEW
*For permission to use
Capsicums, page 5.*
© RBG Kew

· TYPESETTING ·
WYVERN
TYPESETTING LTD

· REPRODUCTION ·
COLOURSCAN
SINGAPORE